The Life and Works of William Wordsworth (1770 - 1850)

A celebration of one of England's greatest poets and the landscapes that he loved.

by Ben Westwood

ISBN 978-0-9564104-5-0

Contains Ordnance Survey data © Crown copyright and database right (2011)

Inspiring Places Publishing
2 Down Lodge Close
Alderholt
Fordingbridge
Hants.
SP63JA

Contents

Below: Blencathra, or Saddleback as it is sometimes known, seen from St. John's Vale. This view would have been very familiar to Wordsworth. He walked this way many times with Coleridge as they journeyed from Dove Cottage to Keswick.

Introduction

William Wordsworth stands as one of the greatest poets of the English language. He considered himself the heir of Chaucer, Spenser, Shakespeare and Milton, and this is far from hubristic. Wordsworth changed the way we read literature. *Lyrical Ballads*, Wordsworth's first and perhaps most famous volume (published first in 1798, and reissued with alterations and revisions in 1800, 1802 and 1805), does no less than attempt to catalyse a revolution in British poetry. The poet makes this abundantly clear in the 1800 'Preface' to the volume, in which he attempts to draw out and realise a kind of poetic creed for the poems that followed:

> They who have been accustomed to the gaudiness and inane phraseology of many modern writers, if they persist in reading this book to its conclusion, will, no doubt, frequently have to struggle with feelings of strangeness and awkwardness; they will look round for Poetry... (Preface to *Lyrical Ballads*: 59)

> And if, in what I am about to say, it shall appear to some that my labour is unnecessary, and that I am like a man fighting a battle without enemies, I would remind such persons, that, whatever may be the language outwardly holden by men, a practical faith in the opinions which I am wishing to establish is almost unknown. If my conclusions are admitted, and carried as far as they must be carried if admitted at all, our judgements concerning the works of the greatest Poets both ancient and modern will be far different from what they are at present, both when we praise and when we censure: and our moral feelings influencing, and influenced by these judgements will, I believe, be corrected and purified. (ibid: 70)

Wordsworth states that his poetry is so different from the poetry the public is used to that it will frequently seem strange and awkward; that a 'practical faith' in the principles of this poetry doesn't yet exist; and that these principles - if they are not subdued by the public's deeply entrenched literary sensibilities - will not only change views of poetry 'both ancient and modern', but correct and purify moral feelings to do with poetry. It is a grand claim, but there is, at this time, a general consensus of remarkable uniformity that the English Romantic poets did indeed shift the focus of poetry for the nation, from the exterior to the interior; from the event to

Daffodils

I wandered lonely as a cloud
That floats on high o'er vales and hills,
When all at once I saw a crowd,
A host of golden daffodils;
Beside the lake, beneath the trees,
Fluttering and dancing in the breeze.
....

For oft, when on my couch I lie
In vacant or in pensive mood,
They flash upon that inward eye
Which is the bliss of solitude;
And then my heart with pleasure fills,
And dances with the daffodils.

'I wandered lonely as a cloud' has been absorbed into the national consciousness to the extent that it ceases to exist solely as poetry anymore, to an extent that the poem itself may struggle to live up to the burden of fame when read in isolation. Reading it as part of Wordsworth's poetry and system of thought leaves little doubt that the poem is snugly tucked away in the midst of Wordsworthian orthodoxy, and though it may not appear to quite merit the extraordinary recognition it receives, it is a clarion declaration of the consolation and comfort open to the clear-sighted receiver of nature.

the individual. There is a reason why readers of this book are more likely to recall a far greater proportion of verse from post-1798 than before the publication of *Lyrical Ballads*. This is because the criteria we used to evaluate poetry changed as a result of the central place of Romanticism in the nineteenth century, and the vast majority of poetry taught in schools illustrates this imbalance.

Whilst the seeds of the revolutionary artistic movement that became Romanticism (which will be discussed later) are to be found in the period preceding Wordsworth, his is so often the name most forcefully and memorably associated with the first 'wave' of Romantic poets that broke upon late eighteenth century Britain, and, it is probably fair to say, rightly so. However, the significance of Wordsworth's name when situated amongst the second tranche of British Romantics (commonly defined as Byron, Keats and Percy Shelley) alters dramatically from the revolutionary author of *Lyrical Ballads*. When Wordsworth took his job as Distributor of Stamps for Westmorland and the Penrith area of Cumberland in 1813, "Wordsworth became an agent of the national revenue-gathering service"(Gill, 1990: 296). Although there is little doubt that Wordsworth was in dire need of the £100 annual salary that came with the position, with a large family to support and little sign of immediate monetary amelioration, no other act of his caused more consternation to the wave of young Romantics. In their eyes the once fiercely radical poet had become a 'Tory hireling', and whilst the decision was almost unavoidably necessary, it was to do the most harm to his reputation as a poet.

This point of Wordsworth's life perhaps best epitomizes both his literary significance, and the multi-faceted contemporary public conception of him. Wordsworth's 'betrayal' was keenly felt by the new-generation Romantics. This in itself encapsulates the complex web of associations that Wordsworth's name holds in its current state. It may suggest to one person the genesis of British Romanticism (itself a far from simple notion), and the accompanying spirit of social rebellion; to another it may signify the worst of Victorian-era rote learning and stuffy conservatism. It may come hand in hand with memories of childhood verse anthologies; or it may seem inextricably linked with the fixed canon of English literature and heavy leather volumes gathering dust in the studies of Oxford English dons.

Whichever Wordsworth one comes to this book with, by its conclusion the reader will, I hope, have been convinced of the importance of the man as both writer and historical figure. He was a man of near unlimited ambition and drive; an absolute (and mostly deserved) confidence in his own ideas and philosophy; and most importantly a man who attempted to change the very heart of a nation, and turn it towards self-knowledge, empathy, and love. There is far too much in the way of history, biographical detail and Wordsworth's own writing to offer a comprehensive account of the man and his work in these pages. Nonetheless, it offers an introduction to the man, his life, and his work, intended to baptise the uninitiated, or to deepen the knowledge and appreciation of those already familiar with the verse. There are certainly plenty of Wordsworthian 'acolytes', but, even for those less zealously inclined, an intimacy with Wordsworth's words and thought cannot help but foster a closeness with nature, and a greater attentiveness to fellow man: it is primarily for this that Wordsworth deserves so fully to be remembered and read.

The Romantic Poets

The name William Wordsworth is synonymous with the movement known as Romanticism, which first appeared (though this is subject to debate) in the eighteenth century, probably in Germany. Up until the mid-twentieth century, in Britain, Romanticism meant six male poets from the late eighteenth to nineteenth century – Wordsworth, Coleridge, Byron, Shelley, Keats, and Blake – but since then the meaning of the word has expanded significantly, so that now when we use the word Romanticism it denotes (not exclusively) "writers, painters, and musicians... [including] Jane Austen, Anna Laetitia Barbauld, William Blake, S. T. Coleridge, John Constable, Franz Josef Hadyn, Leigh Hunt, John Keats, Mary Shelley, Charlotte Smith, J. M. W. Turner, Mary Wollstonecraft, and William Wordsworth" (Roe, 2008: 1). Thomas McFarland characterises aspects which the above artists may concern themselves with as: "a creative interest in ideas and themes that expressed the character of the age: imagination, egotism, the particular, the remote, Greek antiquity, the primitive, the medieval, the East, irrational experiences (including drams and drugs), an awareness of process and current (which extended to new 'organic' conceptions of art), and a longing for the infinite encountered through intense experiences of sublime nature (storms, mountains, the ocean)" (ibid: 5). This list is a useful, if drastically incomplete, account of possible themes one may encounter, and its relevance to Wordsworth's writings will soon become apparent if it is not already.

Though none of the artists mentioned above would have classed or recognised themselves as 'Romantics', any reading of Wordsworth must be contextualised by a knowledge of what is meant by the term. Romanticism grew out of many of the dominant concerns of the previous age, and also contributes to an understanding of the formation of modern Britain – the Romantic spirit has left an indelible mark on our cultural history. However, it was emphatically a pan-European movement across a century or more, and such is the enormous scope of the term that there is only space for the barest of introductions in this book. In fact, the scope of meaning embodied by the word has been a point of discussion and even argument in itself. Some critics have suggested that any term that seeks to group together "the vernacular lyrics of Burns's *Poems Written in the Scottish Dialect* (1786), and the ironic sophistication of Byron's *Don Juan* (1818-24)" (ibid: 8) cannot have a specific enough range of meaning to mean anything at all. One solution to this problem suggested thinking of the word in the plural – referring to Romanticisms instead of Romanticism.

Rather than attempting to capitulate the history of the word, or trace the various attempts of critics to define exactly who fits into the movement, in a few pages, it is more profitable to briefly highlight some areas of Romantic concern with particular relevance to the subject of this book.

Events of revolution, war, and democracy and protest occupied many writers of the time, and Wordsworth was acutely aware of them. The failure of the French Revolution has been seen as an historically crucial aspect of many writers' development and engagement, and Wordsworth was no exception. The following war with France stirred up strong feelings of nationalism (sharpened by the very real threat of invasion in 1797/8 and 1803/4), feelings which captured Wordsworth's imagination – he even enlisted for the army later in life. There was naturally opposition to these stances as well, and Gill lists the massacres of Waterloo and Peterloo as important moulders of Wordsworth's ideals and opinions.

The sublime – the "distinct pleasures in reading about terror and encountering vastness and silence" (ibid: 27) - in nature of course features as a main theme of Wordsworth's poetry, and was a major concern of the age in general. It was a particularly literary concern, but Wordsworth traces it to its source in his encounters with nature, and places it in a thoroughly natural context.

A less contemporary literary influence on much of Wordsworth's writing can be found in the pastoral mode of the Classical world of Greece and Rome. The age's classical inheritance fascinated artists such as Keats, and Benjamin Haydon, and Wordsworth's extensive reading of the 'Greats' allowed him to adapt the pastoral poem to his own surroundings and people, creating the Romantic pastoral.

Sensibility, the most famous treatment of which is to be found in Austen's *Sense and Sensibility*, also features prominently in the imaginative responsiveness to nature and man that is depicted as ideal in the poetry. Writing of sensibility focused on the emotions and human subjectivity, and as such is a key background to tales of rural tragedy such as 'The Ruined Cottage'.

The science and natural science, or philosophy, of the time also forms an important background to Wordsworth's understanding of nature and man. The doubt that had been cast on religion and the existence of God by the emergence of the science of geology, with its revelations that the earth was far, far older than had previously been believed, and was once inhabited by huge creatures now extinct, had a huge effect on both atheists and believers. Indeed, Coleridge's contribution to the debate was an important one, whereby he distinguished between an understanding of Kant's phenomenological world and the imaginative faculty of reason by which the human mind can intuit higher, invisible truths, such as the existence of God. Wordsworth's own theology is closely related to Coleridge's, and the time the two men spent together cannot have been without such discussion and debate.

The above issues, though covered only summarily, will hopefully be enough to awaken an interest in and awareness of key literary and social issues that made up the period of Romanticism – a period which can potentially be contained within Wordsworth's life, and which he bestrides like a colossus even today. There are many excellent guides and introductions to Romanticism, and I strongly recommend that the keen reader goes out and acquires one if they wish to know more about the context of Wordsworth's work, and furthermore about the shaping of our modern national identity and responses to poetry. We are now in an age with significant parallels to Wordsworth's own – 9/11 has had much the same impact in the Western world as the American and French Revolutions had, "then as now, events seemed to have extraordinary, apocalyptic force," (ibid: 2) and the established old order now finds itself nearly surpassed by new world powers. Romanticism may have once meant five or six white male poets of several hundred years ago, but now we can use the word with a much fuller appreciation of its continuing significance, and with a greater understanding of how aspects of this movement not only influenced Wordsworth's writing, but also our own reception of the literature.

*"Come forth into the light of things,
let Nature be your teacher."*
William Wordsworth

Sour Milk Gill, Buttermere

Biography

William Wordsworth was born to John and Ann (née Cookson) Wordsworth on 7 April 1770 in Cockermouth, Cumberland. The second of five children, Wordsworth was born into relative prosperity, though the prosperity was of a fragile and conditional nature, as he would later find out. His childhood abode - "still the most imposing dwelling in the main street of Cockermouth" (Gill, 1990: 14) - belonged in actuality to his father's employer, Sir James Lowther, as did his father John. Lowther, described by Alexander Carlyle as "truly a Madman, tho' too rich to be confin'd" (ibid: 14), pursued his ambition of grasping political control of the North-West with substantial means (gained through both inheritance and marriage) and striking single-mindedness; a fact which, combined with a tactless and tyrannical megalomania (ibid: 14), engendered both hate and fear from the local populace, a feeling unsurprisingly extended to Sir James' law-agent, John Wordsworth.

Stephen Gill doubts, however, that such public enmity towards their father affected Richard, William, Dorothy, John and Christopher unduly in their infant years (ibid: 14). What is likely to have had more effect is the unsettled first five years of his life, shuttled between home and grandparents in Penrith, for reasons unclear. Little formal education occurred until Wordsworth entered Hawkshead Grammar School - an excellent institution which no doubt many would be pleased with today - but, prompted by his father, the young poet did learn long passages of Shakespeare, Spenser and (most importantly) Milton by heart, a practice and power he was to retain until his death in 1850.

The event that was to precipitate Wordsworth's entry into 'beloved Hawkshead' was, however, diametrically opposed to the joyful childhood he was to have there. In 1778 Ann Wordsworth contracted pneumonia and died on 8 March while her children were in Penrith. Soon after Dorothy - William's fondest memory of his infancy and his constant companion from his return home from the continent in 1792 - was sent to live with her mother's cousin Elizabeth Threlkeld, and on 15 May 1779, Wordsworth and his elder brother Richard left their grandparents' house for Hawkshead. Dorothy and William did not see each other again for nine years.

The grammar school at Hawkshead is an important place in Wordsworth's development in three ways. Firstly, the surroundings - places, sights and adventures which were to remain with him throughout his life - which the young Wordsworth had access to began his lifelong obsession (a term which unfailingly appears in almost any account of his life) with

Above: The house of John and Ann Wordsworth, Cockermouth.

nature, and particularly the Lakes. The Vale of Esthwaite was not, in Wordsworth's Hawkshead days, a major part of any itinerary for tourists, and although the Lake District was beginning to become a viable and attractive tourist destination, Esthwaite's main activity came from the still active wool industry, as well as various other concerns local to the Lakes. The adventures of his youth are recounted in invigorating verse in *The Prelude*, where he and his peers roamed over the wild landscape, snaring woodcocks and venturing onto dauntingly high crags as often as they could. The unbridled and perennial appreciation of the natural world so characteristic of Wordsworth's canon surely found hearty nourishment from his days spent exploring the wilderness around Hawkshead.

Secondly, Wordsworth was to find a place that felt like home during his time at the school. Ann and Hugh Tyson boarded boys from Hawkshead from the year Wordsworth began, and he lodged with this loving and generous family until he left for Cambridge in 1787. The security of a fixed and loving domestic centre features as a strong motivation and desire throughout his life, an anxiety stemming partly, perhaps, from his disjointed and nomadic infancy, and from the keenly felt nine-year separation from Dorothy; Ann Tyson provided this centre, and it is clear that Wordsworth, along with his brothers Richard, Christopher and John, felt that he belonged to a real home, with this kind and extraordinary woman "by the strangers to thy blood / Honoured with little less than filial love" (*The Prelude*: IV.19-28).

Thirdly, Wordsworth was to find two tutors in William Taylor and Thomas Bowman who had an enormous impact on his literary development. Whilst Hawkshead prepared students admirably in the standard Cambridge-required subjects of mathematics, science (or Natural Philosophy) and Classics, and whilst Wordsworth was clearly enthralled by his reading of Ovid, Homer, Juvenal and the like, it was the peculiar passion the two masters felt for English literature, both past and contemporary, and their unceasing efforts to provide more than adequate reading material for their students, that stands out as of particular importance to the young Wordsworth. The poet was an avid reader, and devoured everything from contemporary poets such as Crabbe, Gray, and the Wartons, to Newton's *Optics*, but while at Hawkshead (in most first and second-hand accounts around fourteen years of age) (Gill, 1990: 30) he also began to write poetry. His first two publications came in the European Magazine March 1787, which carried the poem 'On Seeing Miss Helen Maria Williams Weep at a Tale of Distress', and lines celebrating the second centenary of Hawkshead. Whilst retaining little interest, even as juvenilia, the date clearly holds some significance, and Wordsworth owed much to the experiments and exercises in verse, as well as the comprehensive and voracious reading, begun as a young schoolboy near Esthwaite.

This important date was, however, once again preceded by tragedy. On 30 December 1783, John Wordsworth died after having been taken ill shortly before Christmas. This bereavement left the Wordsworth children with no permanent home, and little sense of belonging, as well as with approximately £4500 owed to the family in unpaid expenses by Lowther

The grammar school at Hawkshead.

Above: Ann Tyson's cottage in Hawkshead.

which he refused to acknowledge. The legal suit this brought about was not to be resolved until his son, William, became the next Lord Lonsdale upon his father's death in 1804.

The next period in Wordsworth's life, from his start at Cambridge to the end of 1792 could hardly have been more formative and important for him. Entering Cambridge, with the expectation of relatives that he would study diligently and take advantage of the opportunity for 'academic and Church preferment' his contacts afforded, Wordsworth rebelled in spectacular fashion: clandestinely touring revolutionary France largely on foot; fathering a child whilst there; and becoming a fervent radical patriot.

Cambridge, though contemporary accounts are largely unilluminating and Wordsworth's own accounts in *The Prelude* tell us very little in reality, was an unmitigated disappointment for the young man. Compulsory and competitive examinations caused him to recoil, and more general undergraduate anxieties over money, class and loneliness must surely have contributed to a general sense of unease, despite the fact demonstrated by his early confidence in his work that he had "a robust sense of self-worth" (ibid: 39). The natural course of progression after conscientious study at Cambridge was to either the Church or the Law, neither of which appealed to Wordsworth (Richard had entered into the Law; no doubt closing that path definitively for an independent-minded and strong-willed younger brother), and so, after a series of barely intangible hostility towards elder relatives, Wordsworth set off for France for two months in the long vacation of 1790, accompanied by his friend Robert Jones.

The significance of this achievement cannot be underplayed, despite the fact that Wordsworth's French cannot have been good enough to grasp the nuances of political argument and accusation sweeping across the country at the time. The physical details alone make for gruelling reading:

> Between early July and late September 1790
> Wordsworth and his undergraduate friend Robert Jones
> travelled nearly three thousand miles, walking at least two
> thousand of them, many over mountainous terrain, at a rate
> of more than twenty, sometimes more than thirty, miles a day.
> (ibid: 44)

Old habits die hard, and whilst extraordinary to consider, Wordsworth continued to walk with an almost demonic energy until well into his seventies. Often indivisible from Wordsworth's walking and travelling, his literary life also played an important part in the tour, where for the first time he could consolidate his vicarious appreciation of the Alps with first-hand experience. He was not disappointed. The connection between memory, location and literature is a potent one in Wordsworth's canon, and discussion of it should make up a thorough survey of both the poetry and prose.

The period between his return from France and his departure for Dieppe on 26 November 1791 is dealt with in more comprehensive biographies, but suffice to say it was a transitional period for the young Wordsworth, and his second trip to France was to prove even more crucial to an understanding of Wordsworth as a man and poet than the first. Regarding this second trip - a feat of real courage, especially given the volatility of a country convulsed by revolutions and the British government's increasing recourse to near-McCarthyism with the threat of 'sedition' and revolution at home - first in the mind of anyone familiar with Wordsworth's life is the knowledge that sometime in early 1792 Annette Vallon, whom he had likely met at dinner with the family of André-Augustin Dufour, became pregnant with Wordsworth's child, after he had moved from comfortable lodgings in Orléans to Blois, her home town. All that we know for certain about the subsequent course of their relationship is that sometime in September, he and Annette moved back to Orléans. By October, Wordsworth was in Paris, on his way back to England (which he reached by the end of December), having asked Dufour to represent him at the baptism of his daughter, Anne-Caroline Wordsworth, born 15 December. Much about this story is unsatisfactorily vague, as are Wordsworth's motives:

why did he spend over six weeks in Paris while Annette approached her final stages of pregnancy, rather than with her, or in England sorting out his affairs and provisions for his child? Was Wordsworth in love with Annette, and merely distracted by the clear historical import of events in Paris, or was this part of an escape plan that handily coincided with such a charged political time-point? Not enough hard evidence exists - *The Prelude* is almost completely silent about it - and so it is impossible to speculate with any confidence or accuracy. We do know that later in life Wordsworth sustained contact with Annette and his first daughter, Caroline, meeting them in 1802, and in 1812 bestowing an annuity of £30 on Caroline on the occasion of her marriage to Jean-Baptiste Badouin. His wife Mary met Annette for the first time in 1820 in the Louvre, and it is at least clear that Wordsworth never attempted to hide his history with Annette from his family and friends.

Politically, as well as personally, this second trip deepens our understanding of Wordsworth as a young man, and the motivations and emotions which shaped his most famous and important period of activity - 1793-9. An educated and humane French army captain, Michael Beaupuy (1755-96), stands as one of the most important characters of his time in Blois, and Wordsworth offers what Gill describes as "the fullest tribute paid to anyone in *The Prelude*" (IX. 298-328). In Beaupuy, Wordsworth found a man whom 'Man he loved / As man' - a criteria which connects profoundly with the humanitarian concerns of Wordsworth's lyric poetry, where social good is judged on the basic humanity of individual cases, such as 'Simon Lee', or 'Michael', to name but two from many. At a time when Wordsworth found himself in a strange country on the brink of momentous constitutional change as well as on the brink of terrible violence; in a provincial town; with no great command of the language, trying to grasp a political situation which even today remains slippery to define and analyse, Beaupuy's friendship must have been invaluable. Much of Wordsworth's understanding of social frameworks is shaped and presented on a case by case system, and in *The Prelude*, Wordsworth recounts Beaupuy offering what amounts to an almost perfect soundbite when, pointing out two "hunger-bitten" girls in the most awful of situations and saying "Tis against that / Which we are fighting". Such a clear and poetically simple example must have lodged into Wordsworth's memory, as evidenced by his recalling it over a decade later when writing the 1805 *Prelude*. It is also important to mention that, alongside figures such as Beaupuy and the Vallons, his sister Dorothy stands as one of the most important figures of his time on the continent. Both siblings speak joyfully of the possibility of uninterrupted

His friend Thomas De Quincey once estimated that Wordsworth had walked around 180 000 miles during his lifetime, spending many thousands of hours on the Lakeland fells. Walking was a way of life, not simply a means of getting around.
Photo: The Langdale Pikes

"The human mind is capable of excitement without the application of gross and violent stimulants; and he must have a very faint perception of its beauty and dignity who does not know this."
William Wordsworth

residence with each other, and, in a very real sense, to speak of an event occurring to Wordsworth from that point on (if not before), is to speak of it happening to Dorothy as well.

Wordsworth returned from England amidst a political maelstrom, and waded into it by publishing two poems with the famous radical London publisher, Joseph Johnson. 'An Evening Walk' and 'Descriptive Sketches', as well as the marginally later 'A Letter to the Bishop of Llandaff' reveal just how radical Wordsworth's early convictions were. Though Wordsworth was, as the above publications suggest, painfully aware of the broader political and social issues of the time, both he and Dorothy retained an immensely strong affection for each other, and when their wish of a small domestic centre all their own was granted by a generous offer from William Calvert to occupy his farmhouse, Windy Brow, just above Keswick in 1794, they jumped at the chance. Wordsworth, however, despite the publication of a few poems, remained a young man with an illegitimate child in France, with no income, and dependent on the kindness and generosity of a number of people, among them William Calvert, and his son, Paisley.

William and Dorothy moved to Racedown, near Lyme Regis in Dorset, in September 1795, and among the benefits of the move (an enormous library which the Wordsworth's had free access to, and its being located on the stunning Dorset coast) was the proximity of a man whom Wordsworth had met for the first time less than a month before the move, and whose friendship was to be in many ways the defining one of each man's life. Samuel Taylor Coleridge (1772-1834), was known, in 1795, as the author of 'A Moral and Political Lecture', and as a staunch radical causing a stir in political circles, as well as a promising poet. Both Wordsworth and Coleridge played "the civilized eighteenth-century game of open literary allusion" (Gill' 1990: 109), acknowledging poetic debt in public verse, but their friendship quickly became more than this, and, after a period of intellectual activity in which he produced a five-act verse tragedy - *The Borderers* - William and Dorothy moved to Alfoxden House on 4 July 1797, with Coleridge and his wife Sara relatively nearby at Nether Stowey, in north-west Somerset.

Alfoxden was an astonishing piece of luck for the Wordsworths. Its beautiful environs had excited them upon seeing it during a walk, and, largely thanks to a wealthy friend of Coleridge's with some influence in the area - Thomas Poole - a one-year lease was quickly settled on the nine-bedroom mansion. Wordsworth's Alfoxden year proved an immensely important one both personally and poetically, and is bookended by two of his finest poems - 'Lines left upon a Seat in a Yew-Tree' and 'Tintern Abbey'.

Wordsworth, Dorothy and Coleridge were in near constant companionship, frequently walking long distances at odd hours - they would think nothing of setting off on a twenty mile jaunt at four in the afternoon, winter or summer - and the memories of the area and the group's exploration and appreciation of it lasted as ones of a golden period; a period which, to an extent, they were always trying to recreate without absolute success.

Wordsworth's relationship with Coleridge has been the subject of a small forest of published scholarship, and there is no space here for any meaningful discussion of it. Some aspects of Coleridge's literary influence on Wordsworth's canon will be discussed elsewhere in the book, but for now a brief outline of key events in their relationship will hopefully furnish the reader with some information with which to begin their own interpretation of Wordsworth's life and works.

As has been well documented, the 4 October 1798 saw the publication of a volume of poetry entitled *Lyrical Ballads*, published by Joseph Cottle in Bristol (who quickly sold the rights and nearly five hundred unsold copies to J. & A. Arch in London). According to Michael Mason, the book did well critically, though sales were slow. The volume contained about three thousand lines in its first edition (it was re-issued in revised forms in 1800, 1802 and 1805), with around a third of these contributed by Coleridge. Upon the 1800 revision, however, with Wordsworth essentially in charge of the publishing, and, Gill suggests, looking to respond pro-actively to pressing anxieties over his as yet unproven literary reputation, a second volume was added, consisting entirely of Wordsworth's verse, and Coleridge's name was omitted from the title page, leaving Wordsworth as the author. Around this time was also conceived by the two poets the 'plan' for *The Recluse*, a philosophical poem in blank verse, discoursing on 'Nature, Man, and Society'. It was never completed, though it proved to be Wordsworth's own albatross to wear round his neck.

After Dorothy and Wordsworth moved to Grasmere in the Lake District in late 1798, their relationship with Coleridge never returned to the halcyon days of Alfoxden, and various occasions for bitterness and recrimination surfaced intermittently, though no doubt exists as to the very strong affection both parties felt for each other. Coleridge felt Wordsworth had behaved unfeelingly and with a hint of selfishness in the subsequent editions of *Lyrical Ballads*, and to an extent he was right. In Wordsworth's defence, Coleridge - admittedly bad under pressure - had produced very little new poetry of note, and the poetry of Coleridge excised from *Lyrical Ballads* was done with an eye to creating a unity between the artistic creed enunciated in the 'Preface' added to the 1800 edition, and the volume itself.

1803 saw Coleridge, now living in Keswick near the Wordsworth's at Town End in Grasmere, close to physical and mental breakdown. His worsening dependence on opium to alleviate a "compleat and almost heartless Case of Atonic Gout" (Gill, 1990: 221); his sense of self-disgust at his inability to fulfill the role of father and husband; and his artistic drought made him increasingly difficult to live with. Though an at times difficult reunion in 1806 after an absence of two years patched up things superficially, it was not until 1828 and a trip to the continent with Wordsworth's daughter Dora (Dorothy) did Wordsworth and Coleridge really seem to heal old rifts, after a period of palpable coldness and even animosity between the two.

The move to Grasmere indicates another stage in Wordsworth's life - the Lakes were his permanent residence after this date. In 1802 he had married Mary Hutchinson (preceded by the settlement of the Lowther law suit in Wordsworth's favour), who remained his loving and devoted wife till his death, and in 1803 she gave birth to the first of his five children, John, followed by Dora (1804), Thomas (1806), Catherine (1808), and Willy (1810). 1806 saw them move to Hall Farm in Coleorton on an offer from Sir George Beaumont, having been pressed to move to a more spacious home than the tiny Dove Cottage at Grasmere due to the ever-increasing domestic group. George Beaumont and his wife were to prove lasting friends of the family, and Sir George's assent to Wordsworth's request to manage the large grounds at Hall Farm began a love of landscape gardening that led to publications and consultancies later in Wordsworth's life. The large and dynamic domestic group that needed more space included figures such as Mary's sister, Sara, with whom Coleridge became strongly infatuated, Coleridge himself, Thomas De Quincey (a particular favourite of the infant Catherine), and the many guests received by the family at all times of the year. Entertaining was for the Wordsworth's a seemingly natural state of existence, and from contemporary accounts, both from guests and the family themselves, they appear to have welcomed visitors - old friends and awe-struck tourists - with a remarkable hospitality wherever they lived.

In 1808 the family moved again, now to Allan Bank, signalling what was to be a troubled period for Wordsworth and the family. Sales of the 1807 *Poems, in Two Volumes* had been poor; the ill-feeling with Coleridge worsened; Wordsworth suffered from his second bout of eye-disease, keeping him from reading or writing, which would recur intermittently till his death; and the death of his brother John at sea in 1805, which by now had receded into a less immediate grief, was recalled in one of the greatest tragedies the Wordsworth family had to face.

Dove Cottage

On 4 June 1812, whilst Wordsworth was visiting London on business, and Mary with friends in Hindwell, Catherine Wordsworth died, aged three, with neither parent attendant at her death or burial; the illness had been too sudden for news to reach either in time. An additional trial was to come. On 1 December of the same year, their third child Thomas - six and a half years old - died of measles, and was buried next to his sister.

The impact of such events cannot be understated, but it is wrong to imagine that the tragic loss of Catherine and Thomas proved a lasting theme or memory in Wordsworth's verse. Whilst there are unmistakeable notes of stoic resolution in the face of loss in almost all of the poetry published after *The Excursion* (1814), Wordsworth's determination to bear the losses with silent fortitude is remarkable.

The family moved for the final time in May 1813 to Rydal Mount. Along with Alfoxden and Dove Cottage, this residence is one of the three iconic 'abiding places' of Wordsworth and his family. After the publication of *The Excursion*, Wordsworth continued to write and publish, but most of his significant poetry was completed before that year. Wordsworth's reputation did, however, grow steadily despite this, and there are many anecdotes, interesting and amusing, of the consequences of his celebrity. One of the consequences, though, was demand for his presence in the fashionable circles of London society, where he maintained - and began - a number of meaningful friendships. Wordsworth regularly visited London, and stories such as the dinner party at the painter Benjamin Haydon's, with Wordsworth, Charles Lamb, John Keats, and Thomas Monkhouse - where according to Gill's account of Haydon's diary they 'grew uproarious', with Lamb in particular 'the far side of sobriety'- make one wish that more first hand recollections of Wordsworth's time in London existed.

In addition to time in London, and time spent writing, Wordsworth also began campaigning vigorously for the re-election of Sir William Lowther, first Earl of Lonsdale of the second creation (John Wordsworth's employer's son), and, certainly, the Wordsworth of post-1814 appears to have altered in his relative stance towards the British government from the young radical poet who toured revolutionary France. Whilst it is far too reductive to assert that, with age, Wordsworth renounced the radical anti-monarchism of his youth in favour of a rigid, moderate conservatism, and any worthwhile analysis of the course of his political identity would require a whole book, it can be stated with confidence that the older Wordsworth definitely evolved from the younger one.

Wordsworth obsessively revisited and revised his canon, and this was particularly apparent in the editions of his *Collected Works* that had begun appearing in 1815. By the time the third edition had appeared in 1827, Wordsworth was a man beset with worries: Mary, Dorothy and Dora had all been ill; and both John and Willy had in many ways disappointed, or at least given cause for concern. 1833 saw a disease similar to Alzheimer's grip Dorothy - she became increasingly reliant on opium, and was from then on, almost unrecognisable from her former self; refusing to go outdoors, irascible, and extremely difficult to live with. Nonetheless, she was nursed by Mary and Sara as lovingly as is possible, and remained at Rydal Mount with the family. Up until Wordsworth's death in 1850 can be described from then on with some accuracy as his twilight years. Sara Hutchinson died in 1835, followed by a slow procession of friends and acquaintances: Sir Walter Scott, Coleridge and Lamb had all died in the few years prior to that, and though Wordsworth was made Poet Laureate on the death of Robert Southey in 1843, and his daughter Dora married his good friend Edward Quillinan in 1841, Dora's death in 1847 was the last and greatest in a long line of griefs - the third of Wordsworth's children to predecease him. At 12 noon on 23 April 1850, Wordsworth died, having been brought down with pleurisy (perhaps poetically) by a walk in particularly "keen half-snowing cutting north-easterly weather." (ibid: 422)

Rydal Mount where Wordsworth lived from 1813 to 1850.

The Poetry

In discussing Wordsworth's poetry I shall be talking predominantly about two major works: the volume *Lyrical Ballads*, and his autobiographical poem in blank verse (lines of five alternating unstressed-stressed pairs operating without a rhyme scheme), *The Prelude. Lyrical Ballads* - first published in 1798 and then revised, updated and augmented in further versions of 1800, 1802, and 1805 - was the culmination of what is described by many as Wordsworth's annus mirabilis. It was a year bookended by two of Wordsworth's most enduring lyrics - 'Lines left upon a Seat in a Yew-tree' and 'Lines written a few miles above Tintern Abbey' - and a year which saw Wordsworth, Dorothy and Coleridge enjoy a situation of perfect poetic and loving companionship. It is a seminal work in the history of English literature, and the circumstances of its genesis - Wordsworth's hard-nosed practicality and egotism heavily reducing the input of the brilliant but flaky Coleridge - have almost passed into mythology (with the inevitable attendant simplifications and distortions). However, it is also an unstable text. The four different versions of *Lyrical Ballads* all vary from one another, and therefore it is important to remember this when discussing the volume at any length. This book will deal with the 1805 version, unless mentioned otherwise.

The Prelude also has a less than straightforward textual history. Wordsworth never published it in his lifetime - it was published around six weeks after his death in 1850 - and in its modern existence is comprised of three separate texts: the two-book *Prelude* of 1799, and the thirteen- and fourteen-book versions of 1805 and 1850 respectively. Though substantially different in feel, the three recognised versions are not three completely separate texts. Wordsworth was, throughout his life, continually revising and re-imagining his body of verse, and as a consequence the three *Preludes* all have elements of overlap and elements of stark difference. This in itself is an issue demanding reams of academic paper, but suffice it for the purposes of this book that we are aware of the demanding textual issues lurking around the corner during any discussion of his verse. Any good quality edition of the poems will have notes and further reading regarding the editor's decisions and amendments, should one wish to delve deeper into this rich and interesting aspect of Wordsworth's canon.

These two volumes are vital to an understanding of what Wordsworth wanted to achieve through his poetry. *Lyrical Ballads* - and particularly the accompanying 'Preface' added in 1802 - takes its place as "a crucially innovative work from a crucially innovative period of our literature,"

(Mason, 2007: 1) and in *The Prelude* one finds Wordsworth's own account of the growth of his own poetical mind, and by extension an evaluation of his own thoughts about poetry.

The 'Preface' to *Lyrical Ballads* forms something of a manifesto and justification for the new and strange (a key word in Wordsworth's own discussion of the volume) poetry that is offered to the public in the text, and Stephen Gill assesses Wordsworth's aim thus:

> For fundamental human concerns, the 'great and simple affections of our nature', and for a permanently valid language, man must turn not to the polite world of refined manners and educated speech but to the world of Simon Lee, The Brothers, and Michael... For him [Wordsworth] poetry was a moral agent or it was nothing. By loosening the hold of expectation as to what was appropriate subject-matter and treatment for this particular genre (and in the future for others), Wordsworth hoped to arouse readers' imaginations and thus release into the world one grain more of intellectual and spiritual activity. (Gill, 1990: 189)

'The Preface' is a wandering argument, full of clauses and justifications, but, as Gill asserts, its general aim is clear. Wordsworth saw the poems - even as an inherent part of their existence - as social statements:

> Aristotle, I have been told, hath said, that Poetry is the most philosophic of all writing: it is so; its object is truth, not individual and local, but general, and operative; not standing upon external testimony, but carried alive into the heart by passion; truth which is its own testimony... (Preface to *Lyrical Ballads*: 73)
> But Poets do not write for Poets alone, but for men. (ibid: 79)

Though a Poet, according to Wordsworth, is in part defined by his ability to respond more powerfully and immediately to emotional and sensory stimuli, a simple call-and-response formulation of feeling leading to a poem is not enough:

> But whatever portion of this faculty [sensibility] we may suppose even the greatest Poet to possess, there cannot be a doubt but that the language which it will suggest to him must,

in liveliness and truth, fall far short of that which is uttered by men in real life, under the actual pressure of those passions, certain shadows of which the Poet thus produces, or feels to be produced in himself.... it will be the wish of the Poet to... let himself slip into an entire delusion, and even confound identity and his own feelings with theirs, modifying only the language which is thus suggested to him, by a consideration that he describes for a particular purpose, that of giving pleasure. (ibid: 72)

Lyrical Ballads attempts to render (with aptness of selection) the "language really used by men; and, at the same time, to throw over them a certain colouring of imagination, whereby ordinary things should be presented to the mind in an unusual way" (ibid: 59); and while this was a contribution to an already discussed issue rather than an opening up of a new one, the 'strangeness' of the poems is defended with the vigour of a man firmly aware and confident of his own opinions. The following passage, quoted earlier, is worth a second visit:

And if, in what I am about to say, it shall appear to some that my labour is unnecessary, and that I am like a man fighting a battle without enemies, I would remind such persons, that, whatever may be the language outwardly holden by men, a practical faith in the opinions which I am wishing to establish is almost unknown. If my conclusions are admitted, and carried as far as they must be carried if admitted at all, our judgements concerning the works of the greatest Poets both ancient and modern will be far different from what they are at present, both when we praise and when we censure: and our moral feelings influencing, and influenced by these judgements will, I believe, be corrected and purified. (ibid: 70)

Whilst the above stance of Wordsworth's seems definitively anti-establishment (Gill sees it as a moment of birth for "the adversarial stance of the true writer - ... figures such as Shelley, Carlyle, Arnold, Morris, D. H. Lawrence, and many others" (Gill, 1990: 197)) it is important to remember that it is not anti-poetry. It is in fact a spirited defence of the poet's continuing relevance to and impact on the modern world.

Though nominally specific to the poems of *Lyrical Ballads*, the 'Preface' includes important links to Wordsworth's wider poetic (and, as suggested above, this also means public) philosophy; the first of which is exactly that - the social aspect to all of Wordsworth's thinking. As he puts it in the 'Preface', "A Poet is a man speaking to men," ('Preface': 71) and it never escaped Wordsworth's attention that he was writing not just to friends and family, but to the world. He was so aware of this fact that on multiple occasions he specifically asked that his letters not survive him, knowing that without his own prohibiting presence, even the most personal of writings would be subjected to public scrutiny.

Wordsworth, despite what popular imagination may hold, was not a man too preoccupied with flowers and clouds to engage with the sociopolitical issues of his day. In fact, as has been suggested in the biography, the "master theme of the epoch" - the French Revolution - left an indelible mark on Wordsworth due to his very active, though not always publicly apparent, investment in it. A few early poems, posthumously published, testify to the strong radical leanings Wordsworth expressed in his youth, and he is unabashed when he looks back at this period of his life in *The Prelude*. Wordsworth and Coleridge's support for the Revolution and their association with known radical activists - at a time when Pitt's government was resorting to draconian near-McCarthyism to stem the tide of revolutionary sedition they imagined to be sweeping the country - actually led to them being the subject of a covert intelligence operation while at Alfoxden. The government agent sent to spy on them confirmed in a report of 11 August that the Alfoxden gang were "definitely 'French people' who rambled most part of the night" (Gill, 1990: 127). Wordsworth responded creatively to sociopolitical discussion throughout his life, with texts such as *The Convention of Cintra* evidence of this, and it should once again be emphasised that Wordsworth saw his engagement with these issues not just as one man's response, but as a Poet's application of his philosophy to problems afflicting the public. It is a philosophy 'general, and operative', rather than impotent and theoretical, as he himself states.

The following discussion of Wordsworth's poetry must be preceded by an elucidation of just what was this philosophy by which he operated, as a proper understanding of it informs and enriches any reading of his verse; transforming poems like 'Simon Lee' from easy sentimentality to meaningful exposition, and raising the very best - 'Tintern Abbey', for example - to new heights.

The Prelude seeks ultimately to establish the mind of man as the most beautiful and divine subject. The exposition of this philosophy is far from straightforward in the poem, and each new reader is likely to come to his or her own conclusions about Wordsworth's precise meanings - if indeed such

Wordsworth's most famous, and best, sonnet from *The River Duddon* sequence captures both the promise of potential, and the fear of failure, presenting the reader with a transcendent hope; that through our actions we may become 'greater than we know'.

Sonnet to the River Duddon

I THOUGHT of Thee, my partner and my guide,
 As being pass'd away.--Vain sympathies!
 For, backward, Duddon! as I cast my eyes,
I see what was, and is, and will abide;
Still glides the Stream, and shall for ever glide;
 The Form remains, the Function never dies;
 While we, the brave, the mighty, and the wise,
We Men, who in our morn of youth defied
The elements, must vanish;--be it so!
 Enough, if something from our hands have power
 To live, and act, and serve the future hour;
And if, as toward the silent tomb we go,
 Through love, through hope, and faith's transcendent dower,
We feel that we are greater than we know.

precision is possible. The following is (hopefully) a helpful point of ingress, rather than a comprehensive summary, and draws as much as is possible direct from Wordsworth's own words.

The books leading up to eleven and onwards (I will be drawing almost exclusively from the latter part of the poem in this discussion) in the *Prelude* function, to an extent, as evidentiary support for the important notion that love of man and love of Nature (not felt exclusively as joy, but also as terror and fear - the sense of the sublime, according to popular eighteenth century poetic belief) fosters a feeling of spiritual love for all of creation. Innate in this spiritual love (Wordsworth uses 'spiritual' and 'intellectual' interchangeably) is a feeling of unity and connectedness with everything else. This love also empowers the Imagination, a power described as "the main central power" (*Prelude* XIII: 289); "reason in her most exalted mood" (XIII: 170); and "the faculty which produces impressive effects out of simple elements" (Mason, 2008: 37). The ascent of Snowdon described in book thirteen, and in particular the total transformation of the scene by a sea of mist, supplies Wordsworth with an analogy to illustrate the workings of the imaginative faculty in one capable of it:

> One function of such mind had Nature there
> Exhibited by putting forth, and that
> With circumstances most awful and sublime:
> That domination which she oftentimes
> Exerts upon the outward face of things,
> So moulds them, and endues, abstracts, combines,
> Or by abrupt and unhabitual influence
> Doth make one object so impress itself
> Upon all others, and pervades them so,
> That even the grossest minds must see and hear,
> And cannot chuse but feel. (XIII: 74-84)

> This is the very spirit in which they (minds capable of Imagination) deal
> With all objects of the universe:
> They from their very native selves can send abroad
> Like transformation, for themselves create
> A like existence, and, when'er it is
> Created for them, catch it by an instinct.
> Them the enduring and the transient both
> Serve to exalt. (XIII: 91-6)

The imagination allows the divine mind to transform and 'exalt' everything - from the mundane to the sublime - and in exalting each object, thought and image beyond its bare, physical existence, one is able to perceive their divine nature; their connectedness with all the rest of God's creation. This of course rests on the pantheistic faith held by Coleridge, and, to a slightly less zealous degree, Wordsworth, being held as axiomatic; the sense of "a motion and a spirit, that impels / All thinking things, all objects of all thought, / And rolls through all things" ('Tintern Abbey': 101-3). By being aware of the divine essence of all things - including oneself - one then is able to attain ultimate faith in God; a faith that comes from an unshakeable sense of being part of God's creation - "the life / Of all things and the mighty unity / In all which we behold, and feel," (*Prelude* XIII: 253-5) allowing a "consciousness / Of whom [we] are, habitually infused / Through every image" (XIII: 108-10).

Crucially, it is this ability to achieve absolute faith - and through it perceive and comprehend the Godhead itself - that makes the human mind inherently divine, and thus more precious and beautiful than anything else. Through the act of imaginative creation, man is simultaneously acting on creation (including himself), and acting as part of creation, and in doing so exhibiting a power which elevates the mind beyond all other subjects.

The account of the divinity of the human mind offered in *The Prelude* was not intended to stand alone. It was Wordsworth's aim that the poem should be what its title (given to the text after his death by Wordsworth's wife) calls it - a prelude - to a greater work, a poem dealing with no less than the entirety of 'Nature, Man and Society', entitled *The Recluse*. The idea was conceived in the intellectual haven of the Alfoxden year by Coleridge and Wordsworth, and was to set forth a complete philosophy of life. However, no such poem exists in Wordsworth's canon, though we do know that certain works were intended as parts of it. This ghost-poem hovers about every discussion of Wordsworth, and it is important to be aware of it, if only to understand its non-existence. Though such a notion would require an entire book devoted to it, it may prove interesting for the reader, during their own experience of the poetry (and indeed prose), to read the whole of Wordsworth's canon as a composite text of *The Recluse*.

The impressive scope of Wordsworth's ambition apparent in the 'Prospectus to The Recluse' (appearing as part of *The Excursion*) gestures towards the issue of his identity and role as a poet in designating the poetic subject as comprehensive and limitless. The poet is to be preacher, historian, political commentator, arbiter of literary good taste, 'Prophet of Nature', and any other role he cares to assume. In the 'Preface' to *Lyrical Ballads*

Wordsworth asks "what is a poet?" and the question proves to be a salient one.

There can be little doubt that Wordsworth considered his role as a poet as a sacred task. He made no secret of his belief that he was Milton's literary heir; the next poet in a line consisting of Chaucer, Spenser, Shakespeare, and Milton, and the equivocation of his position with Milton's - attested to in particular by the tidal swell of allusions to *Paradise Lost* present in *The Prelude* - provides an insight into Wordsworth's view of his poetic identity. He aligns himself with the poet who identified with the seraph Abdiel in *Paradise Lost* as: "faithful found / Among the faithless, faithful only he" (V. 896-7). Wordsworth, the 'Prophet of Nature', portrays himself in sanctified isolation, a lone voice of truth, praying that God will "let my life / Express the image of a better time" (Prospectus, 2: 74-5). The poet would have the reader come to the poetry as to an instructive sacred text. Such an approach may be demanded by the poet, but of course it is up to the reader whether or not to oblige.

Wordsworth's identity as a poet was also necessarily connected to the type of poem he wrote, the majority of which fall into three main categories: lyric, narrative and philosophical. The power of Wordsworth's philosophical verse is not in doubt (despite its 'narrative' *The Prelude* is here considered a philosophical poem) and lyrics such as 'Daffodils' and 'Elegiac Stanzas' have burrowed deep into the public consciousness. However, Wordsworth's narrative poems - poems of real value, such as 'Michael' and 'The Ruined Cottage' - have, outside academic circles, received perhaps less attention. Coleridge, Wordsworth's fellow 'Prophet of Nature' and the most important human influence on his poetry, considered the type of narrative poetry found in parts of *Lyrical Ballads* to be a distraction from - even harmful to - Wordsworth's true calling as the writer of *The Recluse* -

> A Great Work, in which he will sail; on an open Ocean,
> & a steady wind... - great work necessarily comprehending
> his attention & Feelings within the circle of great objects &
> elevated Conceptions - this is his natural Element - the having
> been out of it his Disease. (Gill, 1990: 223)

Coleridge's judgement here is far from accurate. Though works such as 'The Idiot Boy' will most likely not be on anyone's list of essential Wordsworth, the two long narrative poems mentioned above should feature in even the most cursory glance at the poems.

The complicated textual history of 'The Ruined Cottage' -
Wordsworth was revising, rearranging and rewriting significant portions
throughout much of his career - merely hints at this beguiling poem's
charm. Coleridge was entranced when he heard Wordsworth recite it for
the first time, and it retains its haunting quality, whatever text one reads.
It is a poem about poverty, loss, grief and consolation, but it is also about
the education of the mind by Nature. The narrator of the story is a young
man, possibly a poet (the young, naive poet-narrator is a familiar feature
of the narrative poems), traveling with a wise old man - sometimes called
the Pedlar, sometimes Armytage - who together come across the ruins of a
cottage. The guide - both to the narrator and the reader - then recounts the
tragic tale of Margaret, the former owner, whose husband, unable to provide
for his family, left to join the army, and who eventually loses her two young
children, her sanity, and finally her life. We are expected to implicitly trust
the Pedlar - we are informed that he is to the narrator "a friend / As dear to
me as is the setting sun" - and Wordsworth uses this trust to place us in the
same position of education as the narrator, a placement which could be seen
as an example of that sense of divine unity discussed in 'Tintern Abbey' and
The Prelude, among others. When Armytage informs the poet that

> I see around me here
> Things which you cannot see; we die, my Friend,
> Nor we alone, but that which each man loved
> And prized in his peculiar nook of earth
> Dies with him or is changed, and very soon
> Even of the good is no memorial left.
> The Poets in their elegies and songs
> Lamenting the departed call the groves,
> They call upon the hills and streams to mourn,
> And senseless rocks, nor idly; for they speak
> In these their invocations with a voice
> Obedient to the strong creative power
> Of human passion (ll. 67-79)

he is expecting that the reader will also understand the message of the tale,
and how the divine connectedness of man and Nature may console and
assuage transitory griefs. The Pedlar's final words describe the comfort and
the meaning he draws from this unity:

"*For I have learned to look on Nature, not as in the hour of thoughtless youth, but hearing oftentimes the still, sad music of humanity.*"
William Wordsworth

> I well remember that those very plumes,
> Those weeds, and the high spear-grass on that wall,
> By mist and silent rain-drops silvered o'er,
> As once I passed did to my heart convey
> So still an image of tranquility,
> So calm and still, and looked so beautiful
> Amid the uneasy thoughts which filled my mind,
> That what we feel of sorrow and despair
> From ruin and from change, and all the grief
> The passing shews of being leave behind,
> Appeared an idle dream that could not live
> Where meditation was. I turned away
> And walked along my road in happiness. (ll. 513-25)

These passages provide an important gesture toward Wordsworth's ideas about elegy: that memorial of the departed can be found in the space which they occupied and interacted with when alive; and that the 'passing shews of being' leave behind nothing substantial. It is a notion privileging the divine over the corporeal, and a substantial and moving buttress to the philosophy we began to describe above.

'Michael' stands as one of Wordsworth's finest celebrations of the beauty in the quotidian. It begins with the everyday, almost guidebook-esque, "If from the public way you turn your steps / Up the tumultuous brook of Green-head Gill," leading the reader to "a hidden valley" in "utter solitude," where "beside the brook / There is a straggling heap of unhewn stones! / And to that place a story appertains." Once again, the story is told in the past tense - another elegy - and once again the story is precipitated not by a picture, or the specific memory of a person, but a piece of land. But, we are again told, the land is not merely land, but a part of creation that has shared in the life of other parts:

> … these fields, these hills
> Which were his living Being, even more
> Than his own blood - what could they less? had laid
> Strong hold on his affections, were to him
> A pleasurable feeling of blind love,
> The pleasure which there is in life itself. (ll. 74-9)

Wordsworth deliberately underplays the connection - a connection which is an affirmation of life and God - with the land to better allow the indescribable and divine power of the bond to speak for itself. Rather than attempting to outline the exact nature of the passion - a task clearly beyond Michael himself, and therefore unsuitable for the poem - Wordsworth, as he does in his best narrative poems, lets the silences and things left unsaid speak loudest.

Whilst the poem may appear to offer unstinting praise of Michael's fortitude and capacity for love in the face of the loss of his son Luke, and the final line's echo of the first offer a neat enveloping resolution, some critics have pointed out just how indeterminate and inconclusive is Michael's own fate. The reader's view of Michael recedes after Luke's failure to return: no longer do we see first hand the actions of the couple, but are told first that the narrator talked about what happened next with some people who knew him, and then finally informed of what is generally held to have happened next - "'tis believed by all." This narrative zooming out is deliberate, and the fact that the reader should be left uncertain of the accuracy of the tale preceding that moment adds to the richness of the poem, rather than detracting from it. Whilst there is sadly no space for further discussion of this fascinating poem, hopefully the above discussion has provided some awareness of what Wordsworth tried to achieve with some of the poems in *Lyrical Ballads*. Less is often more, and by adopting this attitude Wordsworth allows the poem to comment on the process of remembering, even as it is performing an act of remembrance itself.

It is important to also be aware when trying to get to grips with Wordsworth that for him writing a poem was influenced by the act of remembering. From his childhood the young poet had almost religiously memorised lines of his favourite poetry, and large parts of Shakespeare, Chaucer, Spenser, and in particular Milton must have been floating around his head consistently, not to mention the verses of more modern poets. This is borne out particularly in *The Prelude*. The poem is in an important sense taking over the baton of epic poetry from Milton's *Paradise Lost* and turning the Christian epic into the psychological kunstlerroman (tale of an artist's growth to maturity) (Milton's epic itself having translated the traditional classical epic of martial deeds to a Christian setting). Evidence of Wordsworth's debt to *Paradise Lost* is clear in the dozens of almost verbatim quotations from it, but it is more than mere plagiarism or unoriginality. Wordsworth uses ideas that have been established (and learned) for generations and places them in new contexts, so that he might use their familiarity to explain new and unfamiliar concepts. For example, in describing the inability to see beyond the physical, purely sensory world, Wordsworth adopts Milton's description of hell as "a universe of death," and in doing so eases the reader's process of comprehension by casting the concept as a familiar idea, couched in familiar language. Any good edition of *The Prelude* will be accompanied by notes highlighting and elucidating the allusions and quotations in the text, and a reading of the poem is greatly enhanced by a consideration of the aptness and frequency of such moments. Such consideration reminds the reader of how keenly Wordsworth felt the 'burden of the past' - the pressure to say something not said before by the huge pantheon of literary greats - and his debt to the lineage of poets he felt himself part of. In the view of some critics Milton also played a supporting role in Wordsworth's defence against accusations that in relocating to the remote Lake District he was guilty of taking the selfish and easy option. His accusers believed that a poet of his gifts must be surrounded by the buzz of current events and intellectualism, and that in locking himself away with nature and family his ability would dwindle and fade, or at least be engaged by little and trivial things, rather than the great subjects of the time. 'Home at Grasmere' (intended as part of *The Recluse*) is Wordsworth's rebuttal to these accusations, and in it he suggests that the move is not one of hiding, but a positive move towards an isolation which would allow him to exercise his mental faculties in the total freedom of contemplative solitude. The blind Milton's own seclusion in his residence while writing his major works was the great literary precedent of that idea. Though Wordsworth was by his own admission, moving towards a certain kind of isolation, he visited London regularly throughout his life, cultivating an extensive network of friends there, and in Milton found an example of the hermetic poet engaging in the most universal of all themes of the time - man's relationship to God.

Memory plays a critical part in all of Wordsworth's poetry, whether it is the subject itself (as is often the case) or even simply passively present in snatches of remembered verse found in the poetry. This fact is attested to, perhaps unexpectedly, by what follows one of Wordsworth's most often quoted phrases:

> For all good Poetry is the spontaneous overflow of powerful feeling; but though this be true, Poems to which any value can be attached were never produced... but by a man who... had also thought longly and deeply. ('Preface' to *Lyrical Ballads*: 154-9)

This can come as a surprise to many who have long associated Romantic poetry with 'spontaneous overflow' and 'extempore effusions'. For

Wordsworth, any feeling worthy of being poeticised must also have been thought about extensively, and so any record of such feelings is of necessity an act of remembering.

In the same way that locations bear special poetical significance as tokens of remembrance in 'The Ruined Cottage' and 'Michael', so do the real locations of Wordsworth's life bear special meaning to scholars. Rather than delineating periods of his poetic development by the poems he published at the time, Wordsworth's timeline is marked with reference to his residences; the places he communicated with every day, and which appear in the poems almost as living, breathing entities themselves. It is clear that this is how Wordsworth would have wanted it to be; even when describing moments of time, he attempts to explain it in the language of physical space. The famous passage of *The Prelude* beginning, "There are in our existence spots of time…" is evidence of this. The section in question suggests that certain moments - spots of time - retain a 'renovating virtue', sustaining us in moments of darkness, and ultimately leading us to the rightful position of mind as "lord and master, and that outward sense / Is but the obedient servant of her will" (XI. 271-2). As example Wordsworth provides two specific situations from his childhood that he remembers vividly, and which he believes to have affected him during later life. Describing these moments as partly physical 'spots' - and not just 'moments' - is key to the notion that they are more than just nostalgic reminiscences - that they have a real, measurable impact on the present, and in comprehending the way in which Wordsworth ascribed almost tangible attributes to memories, the reader is able to once again go deeper into the poetry. It may help to dispel any preconceptions or anxieties that one may have about Wordsworth simply being a poet who liked the look of flowers in the spring, and rivers by a mountain. When Wordsworth remembers these sights, sounds, and smells, he is not indulging in empty poeticisms, but attempting to record the effects and processes of remembering; effects he ascribes critical importance to.

An excellent and most likely less well known framing of the issues of memory and location are to be found in a trio of poems written across the span of twenty eight years about the famous Yarrow Water in the Borders region of Scotland: 'Yarrow Unvisited', 'Yarrow Visited', and 'Yarrow Revisited'. Together they form a pleasingly whole picture of the process of imagination and memory visited upon places by Wordsworth's mind. In the first poem the prospect of a visit to Yarrow is dismissed - "why waste a needful day / To go in search of Yarrow?" However, the poet's bluffness gradually warms, leading first to an image of the "sweets of Burn-mill

Photo: The stepping stones over the River Duddon near Seathwaite.

The Stepping Stones by William Wordsworth

The struggling rill insensibly is grown
Into a brook of loud and stately march,
Crossed ever and anon by plank or arch;
And, for like use, lo! what might seem a zone
Chosen for ornament,—stone matched with stone
In studied symmetry, with interspace
For the clear waters to pursue their race
Without restraint. How swiftly have they flown,
Succeeding,—still succeeding! Here the child
Puts, when the high-swollen flood runs fierce and wild,
His budding courage to the proof; and here
Declining manhood learns to note the sly
And sure encroachments of infirmity,
Thinking how fast time runs, life's end how near!

'The Stepping Stones' calls to mind both the 'glad preamble'
of the poet's youth described in The Prelude, and the sombre,
elegiac mood of 'Yarrow Unvisited' and 'Extempore Effusion',
consolidating life's entire journey into one moment of reflection.

meadow," and finally to an assertion that Yarrow must be left "unseen, unknown! / It must, or we shall rue it: / We have a vision of our own; / Ah! why should we undo it." The poet's imagination has created an idyll in the as yet memorially vacant space of Yarrow, and as an unblemished image it will be a source of future consolation by virtue of its perfection and by the fact that in Yarrow Unvisited there will remain at least one beautiful thing in the world left to see.

'Yarrow Visited' does not offer as much as either of the two poems flanking it; its function is to confirm the truth of the poet's vision of a place of beauty (a place given special meaning as much by remembrance of the stories attached to the landscape as its natural beauty), and changes the nature of the consolation offered by the memory-location. 'Yarrow Revisited' draws on both the reader's and Wordsworth's own familiarity with the location in order to use it now as an elegy-in-location, just like the 'Ruined Cottage', and the heap of stones in 'Michael'. This time Wordsworth treats himself as the poetic subject, contrasting the unchanged nature of the location against the work of time on himself and his companions, striking a sombre and beautiful elegiac note.

The remembrance of man in location proves a powerful consolation in any number of instances throughout Wordsworth's poetry - three particularly moving examples being the poems after the death of his brother John at sea, addressing a daisy inhabiting the last place Wordsworth saw him: 'To the Daisy (Sweet Flower!)'; 'I only looked for pain and grief'; and 'Distressful gift! this Book receives'. The location retained a powerful hold over Wordsworth - it was recorded that he was able to identify the precise spot well into his later years. The importance of the memories in locations discussed above is, in my opinion, absolutely essential to any reading of the poetry; however, it is also useful to note that it was not simply static physical locations that are the vessels, but every part of creation. An interesting example of this may be found in 'The Old Cumberland Beggar', whereby the eponymous vagrant is himself a living, breathing memorial to the "small, unremembered acts of kindness" performed to him every day, that otherwise would be forgotten completely.

As mentioned at the beginning of this chapter, Wordsworth saw poetry as socially instructive, and an account - however brief - of his poetry would be remiss if it did not mention the special concerns he had for the poetry's educational aspect, and education in general. The late eighteenth century leading into the Victorian era was a time with an ardent interest in theories of education - Wordsworth and Coleridge themselves ascribed to the popular 'Madras', or Monitorial, system of instruction. Wordsworth felt keenly the advantage of his excellent education at Hawkshead, and, upon becoming concerned with his eldest son's education, decided to home-school him; disastrously, Gill reports. Despite this failure to translate his own learning experience into a mode of education for his child, Wordsworth's many passages dealing with both his own childhood and others ('To H. C., Six Years Old' being an excellent example) should be read in the light of the poet's passionate engagement with the issue of childhood education.

I hope this section will have given the reader an insight into Wordsworth's own ideas about his identity as a poet, and an adequate account of the wider 'philosophy' guiding the works, the articulation of which was the dominant, but unachieved, aim of his life. A knowledge of the beliefs Wordsworth held can enrich a reading of the poems; and provide a fresh perspective with which to look at familiar poems in a new light, using the importance of the idea of memory as a new lens for the reader already at home with the works of the great 'Prophet of Nature'.

"Poetry is the spontaneous overflow of powerful feelings: it takes its origin from emotion recollected in tranquility."
William Wordsworth

Derwentwater

Ullswater - "It is the happiest combination of beauty and grandeur, which any of the lakes affords". William Wordsworth

The Guide to the Lakes

In 1809 Wordsworth was approached by an old acquaintance -
Joseph Wilkinson, Rector of East and West Wretham in Norfolk - who
was working on a book of drawings of the Lake District, and was asked if
he or Coleridge would provide text to accompany the views. Wordsworth
was attracted, no doubt, by the opportunity firstly to begin a work that
'had been waiting to be written'; secondly by the chance to produce a fully
informed riposte to the huge number of fashionable Lake District guide
books that had exploded in popularity in the latter half of the eighteenth-
century; and thirdly by a desperately needed accompanying fee. Wilkinson's
book, entitled *Select Views in Cumberland, Westmoreland, and Lancashire*,
sold tolerably well, but in 1835 Wordsworth published the text in a stand
alone volume entitled *Guide to the Lakes*, which proved to become "the
other volume (along with *The Excursion*) of his most often packed in
knapsacks." (Gill, 1990: 234)

Stephen Gill claims the *Guide* offers "by far Wordsworth's most
accessible prose", and is a pleasure to read, regardless of one's location.
The vision Wordsworth presents in the book is one of a harmonious and
symbiotic community of extraordinary natural beauty, albeit a community
whose stability and splendour was under threat from the dangers of mass-
tourism and development. Indeed, a whole section of the book is dedicated
to this very topic, entitled 'Changes, and Rules of Taste for Preventing Their
(tourists') Bad Effects'. Despite this, though, the text always brims with a
sincere admiration, fondness, and awe, rather than descending into hateful
polemic - Wordsworth emphasises himself that the only way to adequately
appreciate the scenery is to come to it ready and willing to be delighted,
rather than with preconceptions or comparative subjects.

It is not only with the touristic invasion of his home county - with all
the accompanying destruction - that Wordsworth used the *Guide* to address;
to him, an inhabitant of the Lakes for all but three years of his life, the
guides currently available came from faulty sources of knowledge. No one
would have been more qualified to write a walking companion to the Lakes
than Wordsworth. He states right at the beginning of the text that:

> It is hoped, also, that this Essay may become generally
> serviceable, by leading to habits of more exact and considerate
> observation than, as far as the writer knows, have hitherto
> been applied to local scenery. (*Guide to the Lakes* (ed. de
> Sélincourt), 2004: 41)

This wonderful moment of classically Wordsworthian egotistical certainty captures another important point about the Guide. Exact and considerate observation is exactly what he exemplifies in all the book's descriptive passages, and he states that:

> It is upon the mind which a traveller brings along with him that his acquisitions, whether of pleasure or profit, must principally depend. (ibid: 98)

As with all of his writings, the text is inescapably an instructional one; when Wordsworth describes the quality of the shifting light across the Vale of Esthwaite on an autumnal midday, he is not only describing why it is beautiful, but also how we should likewise enjoy it. For example:

> It has been said that in human life there are moments worth ages. In a more subdued tone of sympathy may we affirm, that in the climate of England there are, for the lover of Nature, days which are worth whole months, - I might say - even years. One of these favoured days sometimes occurs in spring-time... But it is in autumn that days of such affecting influence most frequently intervene; - the atmosphere seems refined, and the sky rendered more crystalline, as the vivifying heat of the year abates; the lights and shadows are more delicate; the colouring is richer and more finely harmonized; and, in this season of stillness, the ear being unoccupied, or only gently excited, the sense of vision becomes more susceptible of its appropriate enjoyments. (ibid: 59)

Wordsworth's reference to a poem on the first of May written by Buchanan emphasises the folly and incomplete knowledge of other guide book authors, and the whole passage states as objective fact what is most beautiful in autumn. The frequently sublime peaks that the prose in the Guide hits however prevent these statements from grating, as the writing above (and further passages below) indicates. Many examples of these moments may in fact be found amusing by the modern reader, as, for example, when Wordsworth states that, "nor will the singular beauty of the chimneys escape the eye of the attentive traveller;" or when he laments - with something of the staunch conservatism he is almost famous for - over the immigrant larch's inferiority to the 'native' foliage that it has so often supplanted. Ernest de Sélincourt's introduction to the text highlights this

St. John's Vale and the crumbling blue-grey weathered 'schist', more properly slate, so typical of Cumbrian mountains. How much more inspiring would Wordsworth have found these landscapes had he known of the global tectonic movements which had built these volcanic ___

'fine extravagance' by pointing out the inconsistency in Wordsworth's admiration of the likewise 'foreign' sycamore, and asking when the larch will be accorded the same honorary status of resident. Nonetheless, this does not detract from the validity and genuineness of the book's content. Both de Sélincourt and Gill point out the earnest sincerity within, and its value both as further statement of his convictions about man and Nature and as a beautiful piece of writing in its own right more than justify time spent delving into its small hoard of treasures, whether avid Wordsworthian or keen rambler, literary-minded passer-through or uninitiated tourist. However, it is likely that the average reader will not have a copy of this book lying around the house, and, while I would particularly urge those visiting the Lakes to procure a copy for themselves, it makes a great deal of sense at this point to allow Wordsworth's inspiring and informed prose a little space to speak for itself.

> In the ridge that divides Eskdale from Wastdale, granite is found; but the MOUNTAINS are for the most part composed of the stone by mineralogists termed schist, which, as you approach the plain country, gives place to lime-stone and free-stone; but schist being the substance of the mountains, the predominant colour of their rocky parts is bluish, or hoary grey - the general tint of the lichens with which the bare stone is encrusted. With this blue or grey colour is frequently intermixed a red tinge, proceeding from the iron that interveins the stone, and impregnates the soil. The iron is the principle of decomposition in these rocks; and hence, when they become pulverized, the elementary particles crumbling down, overspread in many places the steep and almost precipitous sides of the mountains, with an intermixture of colours, like the compound hues of a dove's neck. (ibid: 45)

> 'I observed,' says he, 'the beautiful effect of the drifted snow upon the mountains, and the perfect tone of colour. From the top of the mountains downwards a rich olive was produced by the powdery snow and the grass, which olive warmed with a little brown, and in this way harmoniously combined, by insensible gradations, with the white...'
> (ibid: 47)

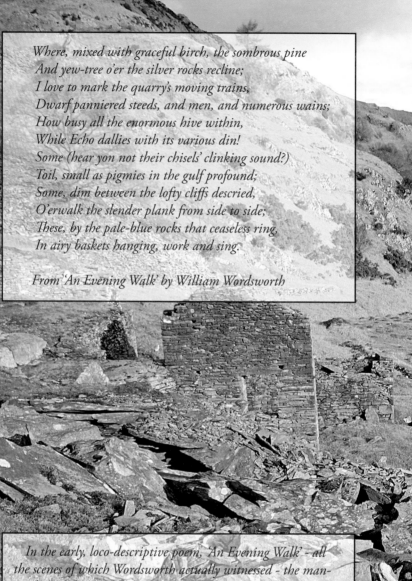

Where, mixed with graceful birch, the sombrous pine
And yew-tree o'er the silver rocks recline;
I love to mark the quarry's moving trains,
Dwarf panniered steeds, and men, and numerous wains;
How busy all the enormous hive within,
While Echo dallies with its various din!
Some (hear yon not their chisels' clinking sound?)
Toil, small as pigmies in the gulf profound;
Some, dim between the lofty cliffs descried,
O'erwalk the slender plank from side to side;
These, by the pale-blue rocks that ceaseless ring,
In airy baskets hanging, work and sing.

From 'An Evening Walk' by William Wordsworth

In the early, loco-descriptive poem, 'An Evening Walk' - all
the scenes of which Wordsworth actually witnessed - the man-
made and the natural are simply, but gracefully, conflated, and
distinctions between the two become difficult to draw. The clink
of chisels rebound off the landscape, and the scene itself becomes
more powerfully remembered because of its assimilation into
the natural landscape.

Photo: Part of the old slate quarry at Tilberthwaite.

The connection Wordsworth felt with the area was - as is evidenced in every line of his writing - a deeply spiritual one. Familiar themes are easily recognised in the descriptions of the natural and universal harmony of man and Nature -

> Hence buildings, which in their very form call to
> mind the processes of Nature, do thus, clothed in part with
> a vegetable garb, appear to be received into the bosom of
> the living principle of things, as it acts and exists among the
> woods and fields. (ibid: 71)

Furthermore in its appreciation of the small and humble cottages, symbolic of the shared life of the inhabitants and their environment, with all their small daily concerns and labours, and in stark opposition to the gaudy and (in Wordsworth's eyes) obtrusively ugly mansions set atop the highest hills and commanding the best views. Such an hubristic approach to architecture, he asserts, can only come a distant second best to Nature's own majestic promontories. Also emphasised is the healing power of Nature - the sense of absolute and divine calm one feels when in the presence of works of great natural beauty; that "placid and quiet feeling" which so often provides consolation to the narrator in his poems.

It stands in clear relation and kinship to Wordsworth's other works, and, as has been pointed out, if not for "the utilitarian connotations of 'guide' it would be recognized more freely what it is, a gem of Romantic writing." (Gill, 1990: 284) However, the connotations of guide are not entirely wasted - the details, hints, itineraries and suggested excursions are remarkably detailed, and the text itself - as illustrated by the passages quoted above - cannot but help enhance any scene the reader may recognise from the book. In fact, throughout the book the reader may feel occasionally a strange sense of déja vu, where descriptions of certain places and features (the islands on lakes, for example) remind the reader of events described in *The Prelude*, or elsewhere in his verse. The sensation is an uncanny one, and is testament to Wordsworth's extraordinary powers of evocative description.

Any guide or visit to the Lake District would not be complete without the presence of the infamous rain. However, unsurprisingly, Wordsworth sees the weather differently to how it is commonly portrayed, and it is perhaps fitting to conclude this section with his views on the matter:

> It may now be proper to say a few words respecting
> climate, and 'skiey influences,' in which this region, as far as
> the character of its landscapes is affected by them, may, upon

the whole, be considered fortunate. The country is, indeed, subject to much bad weather, and it has been ascertained that twice as much rain falls here as in many parts of the island; but the number of black drizzling days, that blot out the face of things, is by no means proportionally great. Nor is a continuance of thick, flagging, damp air so common as in the West of England and Ireland. The rain here comes down heartily, and is frequently succeeded by clear, bright weather, when every brook is vocal, and every torrent sonorous… Such clouds, cleaving to their stations, or lifting up suddenly their glittering heads from behind rocky barriers, or hurrying out of sight with speed of the sharpest edge - will often tempt an inhabitant to congratulate himself on belonging to a country of mists and clouds and storms, and make him think of the blank sky of Egypt, and of the cerulean vacancy of Italy, as an unanimated and even a sad spectacle.(*Guide to the Lakes* (ed. de Sélincourt), 2004: 58)

Even on 'black drizzling days' the sun frequently breaks through and illuminates the landscape.

"Where Derwent rests, and listens to the roar
That stuns the tremulous cliffs of high Lodore;"
William Wordsworth - 'An Evening Walk'

Lodore Falls, by Derwentwater, the
subject of a poem by Wordsworth's
friend Robert Southey.

In Conclusion

Wordsworth's later years were undoubtedly lesser in poetical output – both quantity and quality – and it is right that the main focus of a book about Wordsworth's life and poetry in general should be the earlier years. However, these later years were not without their great moments. The manifold griefs of the years took their toll: deaths of peers and friends, as well as two children (eventually three) who predeceased him, and Dorothy's awful illness which left her, in Wordsworth's own words, 'my poor, ruin of a sister'; and yet, they culminated in one of Wordsworth's very finest poems, and – in Stephen Gill's judgement – his best elegy. This poem, 'Extempore Effusion upon the Death of James Hogg', reproduced in part below, is too long for a full discussion here, but it speaks as eloquently for Wordsworth's own remembrance as the friends it commemorates by name:

> The mighty Minstrel breathes no longer,
> Mid mouldering ruins low he lies;
> And death upon the braes of Yarrow
> Has closed the Shepherd-poet's eyes:

> Nor has the rolling year twice measured,
> From sign to sign, its steadfast course,
> Since every mortal power of Coleridge
> Was frozen at its marvellous source;

> The rapt One of the godlike forehead,
> The heaven-eyed creature sleeps in earth:
> And Lamb, the frolic and the gentle,
> Has vanished from his lonely hearth.

> Like clouds that rake the mountain-summits,
> Or waves that own no curbing hand,
> How fast has brother followed brother,
> From sunshine to the sunless land!

> Yet I, whose lids from infant slumbers
> Were earlier raised, remain to hear
> A timid voice that asks in whispers,
> 'Who next will drop and disappear?'

Our haughty life is crowned with darkness,
Like London with its own black wreath,
On which with thee, oh Crabbe! Forth-looking,
I gazed from Hampstead's breezy heath.

As if but yesterday departed,
Thou too art gone before; but why
O'er ripe fruit, seasonably gathered,
Should frail survivors heave a sigh?

Mourn rather for that holy Spirit,
Sweet as the spring, as ocean deep;
For Her who, ere her summer faded,
Has sunk into a breathless sleep.

Wordsworth here writes as meaningfully and beautifully about death as he does about life, and the poem is a wonderful snapshot of the poet's attitude of empathy, love, fortitude, and above all the preciousness of life. In fact, it is, perhaps, in the inextricable link between life and poetry in the verse that some of the core strength of Wordsworth can be found. Though far from superficial, he was happy to embrace the simplicity of the outer life to uncover the beauty and complexity of the inner. Despite the fact that occasionally Wordsworth's poems will show their age, the essential vitality afforded them by this bond with real life lets them almost always speak to the universal. Though, as Wordsworth quite rightly suggests, the type of man portrayed in 'The Old Cumberland Beggar' no longer exists in that particular form in our own society, the sentiments of the poem retain meaning and power, because they are founded on a perennial fixture of humanity – the person in need. This is true of all great poetry, but Wordsworth's inimitable verse locates this universality in the everyday; and so while the language of the poems may appear simultaneously lofty and alienating, and quotidian and uncouth, it only requires a little contextualising, and a little guiding, in order to enjoy the poems as they were intended.

The debt owed to Wordsworth by a multitude of succeeding writers is extensive:

Tennyson's great elegy 'In Memoriam' (1850) learned from Wordsworth... Ezra Pound's modernist slogan 'make it new' was a Romantic idea, updated from the *Preface to Lyrical*

Ballads; James Joyce's 'epiphanies' in *Dubliners* and *A Portrait of the Artist as a Young Man* resembled the 'spots of time' on which Wordsworth's *Prelude* was structured... Seamus Heaney's poems about childhood such as 'Death of a Naturalist' and 'Personal Helicon' are thoroughly Wordsworthian in manner. (Roe, 2008: 8)

Frederick Denison Maurice puts it another way,

> Wordsworth's *Prelude* seems to me the dying utterance of the half century we have just passed through, the expression – the English expression at least – of all that self-building process in which, according to their different schemes and principles, Byron, Goethe, Wordsworth, the Evangelicals (Protestant and Romanist), were all engaged, which their novels, poems, experiences, prayers, were setting forth, in which God, under whatever name, or in whatever aspect He presented Himself to them, was still the agent only in fitting them to be world-wise, men of genius, artists, saints. (Abrams et al, 1979: 560)

and it is absolute testament to Wordsworth's enduring power that he should be both the final voice of the first half of the nineteenth century (in a poem published posthumously), an example for the famed poet laureate who dominated the second half, and a touchstone for the modernists who sought to revolutionize literature again in the twentieth century. It is the same enduring power that allowed the man to climb Helvellyn at seventy years of age, and the same power which makes 'I wandered lonely as a cloud' probably the most famous line of English poetry.

If all that was left of Wordsworth was a sparsely detailed biography, he would be a figure whose remarkable vigour and determination to fulfil his vocation as poet and inhabitant of earth as earnestly as possible stood as worthy of admiration alone. Luckily, we are also in possession of thousands and thousands of words of poetry and prose, an autobiography in verse, Dorothy's journals and letters, and dozens of accounts of meetings with the man from figures such as Matthew Arnold, William Hazlitt, Algernon Swinburne, and John Ruskin, as well as libraries worth of scholarship, both professional and amateur. The above material amounts to more than enough to confirm, through our own objective judgement, Coleridge's simple assessment of the man written to a friend early in the two poets' acquaintance: **Wordsworth is a great man.**

"I listened, motionless and still;
And, as I mounted up the hill,
The music in my heart I bore,
Long after it was heard no more,"
William Wordsworth

The photograph shows the village and lake at
Grasmere where Wordsworth lived at Dove Cottage.

A brief guide to "Wordsworth country".

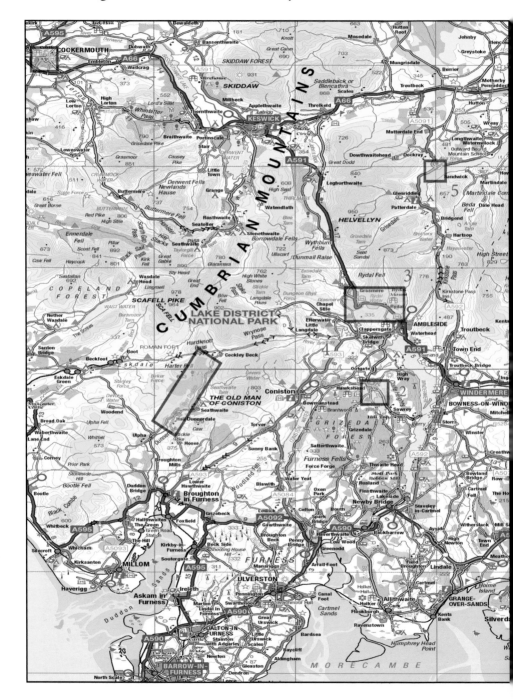

The map left highlights some of the main Lakeland sites associated with William Wordsworth. They are as follows:

1.	Cockermouth - the house where Wordsworth was born is on the main street in Cockermouth. It is owned by the National Trust and in 2011 was open everyday except Fridays from 12th March to the end of October.

2.	Hawkshead village. The grammar school attended by Wordsworth is now a museum and is open every day from April 1st to the end of October. The home of Anne Tyson where Wordsworth lodged is in the village and is now a holiday cottage.

3.	Grasmere and Rydal. Dove Cottage where Wordsworth and his sister Dorothy lived from 1799 to 1808 is in the village of Grasmere. It is open most days of the year (check website) and is owned by the Wordsworth Trust. There is also a museum. Rydal Mount, Wordsworth's last home, in nearby Rydal is also open to the public, daily from March 1st to the end of October and Wednesday to Sunday, November, December and February.

4.	The valley of the River Duddon, a favourite location of Wordsworth.

5.	Ullswater near the mouth of Aira Beck, where daffodils inspired Wordsworth to write his most famous poem.

Below: The simple graves of William Wordsworth, his wife Mary, sister Dorothy and other family members in the churchyard at Grasmere.

"Dora's Field" by Rydal Mount. This field was originally bought by Wordsworth to build a house for his daughter Dorothy. When she died in 1847 he planted hundreds of daffodils as a memorial. It is now owned by the National Trust.

Bibliography

Primary sources:

Abrams, M. H., & Gill, S., & Wordsworth, J., eds. (1979), The Prelude 1799, 1805, 1850, London.

De Selincourt, E., ed. (2004), Guide to the Lakes, London.

Gill, S., ed. (2008), William Wordsworth, The Major Works including The Prelude, Oxford. (All references from The Prelude refer to the 1805 edition.)

Mason, M., ed. (2007), Lyrical Ballads (2nd ed.), London.

Wu, D., ed. (2009), Romanticism: An Anthology (3rd ed.), Oxford.

Biography:

Gill, S., (1990), William Wordsworth: A Life, Oxford. Contains excellent extended bibliographies for suggestions of further reading.

Secondary sources:

Abrams, M. H., (1971), Natural Supernaturalism, London.

Glen, H., (1983) Vision and Disenchantment: Blake's Songs & Wordsworth's Lyrical Ballads, Cambridge.

Lindenberger, H., (1963), On Wordsworth's Prelude, Princeton.

Roe, N., ed. (2008), Romanticism: An Oxford Guide, Oxford. Again, comprehensive introduction to Romanticism, and full of further reading suggestions.